Original title:
Life's Big Questions in 140 Characters or Less

Copyright © 2025 Creative Arts Management OÜ
All rights reserved.

Author: Vivienne Beaumont
ISBN HARDBACK: 978-1-80566-158-0
ISBN PAPERBACK: 978-1-80566-453-6

The Search for Meaning

Why's the sky blue, I ask with glee?
Is it paint or a cosmic decree?
Why do cats stare, plotting a heist?
And why does my fridge hum, like it's iced?

Shadows of Tomorrow

Will tomorrow bring pizza or more pain?
Should I worry or just dance in the rain?
Will aliens steal my sandwich, oh dear?
And why do I lose socks, year after year?

What Lies Beyond the Horizon?

Do clouds hold secrets or just plain fluff?
Is there Wi-Fi up there, or is it tough?
What if the sun just wants to play?
And the moon's a giant, shy soufflé?

Canvas of Dreams and Doubts

I paint my hopes in colors bright,
But spill my doubts in the dead of night.
Is that a masterpiece, or just a mess?
In the realm of chaos, who can guess?

Breaths of Infinite Possibility

Is it cake or is it real?
Guess I'll just have to kneel.
In this world of endless fun,
Every quest has just begun.

Why is the sky always blue?
And why can't socks find their crew?
Questions dance like butterflies,
Tickling our curious eyes.

Can a cat truly rule the day?
Or will the dog have its say?
Let's debate in playful jest,
For whims are what we love best.

What's the meaning of a smile?
Is it just a fleeting style?
Let's laugh until we find out,
In this giggle-filled route!

The Puzzle of Existence

Why are we here, you ask with glee?
To drink bad coffee and watch TV.
Existence's a riddle, oh what a jest!
Yet we keep searching for the ultimate quest.

Some say it's love, others say fame,
While squirrels just dance, and never feel shame.
A puzzle with pieces that never quite fit,
Maybe it's simply to laugh and to sit.

Are Questions Just Reflections?

Mirror, mirror, on the wall,
Do you hear my frantic call?
Is there wisdom in your glass?
Or just that hair I forgot en masse?

Inquiries swirl like leaves in the air,
Is asking too much, or just a dare?
Reflections of thoughts, so wacky and absurd,
Are we just parrots, repeating each word?

The Firefly's Secret Quest

A firefly flickers, a tiny light,
Searching for answers deep in the night.
What's the purpose of this shiny glow?
Does it find love, or just bugs to stow?

With each little blink, it asks so sly,
"Do trees have feelings? Do stars ever cry?"
Secret quests beneath the moonbeam's hue,
Maybe we're all just fireflies too.

The Intersection of Wonder and Doubt

At a crossroads, I pause, confusion in tow,
Do I turn left for answers or right for the show?
Wonder leads to joy, while doubt feels like slime,
Can I get both on a single dime?

In the circus of thoughts, I juggle and toss,
Should I worry about winning, or bask in the gloss?
Each question a jester, each answer a clown,
In this big top of thoughts, can I wear a crown?

Do We Walk in Circles?

Round and round, are we all lost?
Paths we take, always the cost.
Heads held high, yet feet in grime,
Finding answers through endless mime.

Each step a question, each laugh a clue,
Tangled thoughts in a dance we do.
Am I right? Or am I confused?
Chasing tails; by life we're amused.

Thresholds of Change

One foot in, one foot out,
Change is scared; it's full of doubt.
Do I leap? Or play it safe?
Like a cat, can I find my waif?

Jump that line, or sip my tea?
What's the formula to be free?
Pick a door, close my eyes tight,
Maybe there's cake, or a frightful sight!

Dreams Painted on the Canvas of Night

Night's the stage where odd things play,
Brush strokes bright, then fade away.
Monsters dance, and stars make noise,
Life's sketchbook harbors girlish joys.

Pillow talks with shadows deep,
Twisted tales that never sleep.
Doodling hopes with a pen so bold,
In dreams we laugh, in dreams we fold.

When Will the Answers Be Clear?

Peering through a sticky glass,
Each reflection hides the sass.
Answer buttons on a wonky board,
Push one; get a free dessert reward!

Tick-tock asked the anxious clock,
While mice play chess on a soapbox.
Maybe when pigs sprout some wings,
Only then will we find the things.

Bridges to the Unknown

Why do socks disappear?
It's like magic in the dryer.
Is a sneeze a mini-explosion?
Or just your nose being a liar?

What if dogs see us as gods?
Throw a ball, they'll obey.
Do they believe they control us?
It's quite the canine play!

Is pizza a vegetable?
If you squint, it might make sense.
Pizza health claims on the rise,
With every slice, we convince!

Why do we all avoid the truth?
Is denial a warm embrace?
Or just a game we play with time,
A funny little race?

The Dance of Fate and Free Will

Do we write our own script?
Or is it already penned?
Are choices just a fun charade?
A game with no true end?

If I flip a coin today,
Will it change my destiny?
Or just land back in my palm,
To mock my sanity?

Why do we laugh at our fears?
Is humor life's best guide?
When the world seems upside down,
I chuckle and can't hide!

Do we dance or just stumble?
With fate leadin' the way?
In a twirl of bizarre moments,
We laugh as we sway!

Ciphers of the Heart

Why do crushes feel like puzzles?
Confusion wrapped in glee.
Do they take a special code?
To unlock you and me?

Is love just a TikTok trend?
Or an ancient cast spell?
Swipe left, or swipe right, my friend,
In social realms we dwell!

If hearts can be a cipher,
What message do they send?
A code that baffles the brain,
Yet makes us want to blend?

When flirts become a circus,
Do clowns win hearts or roar?
Maybe laughter is the key,
To love and so much more!

Kaleidoscope of Questions

Is the universe a big joke?
Or just a cosmic play?
If we laugh, do stars laugh back?
What do they do all day?

Can cats see spirits of night?
Or are they just aloof?
Do they ponder on their purrs?
Or is it all just fluff?

What if tomorrow's just a myth?
And today, the only show?
Should we eat dessert first then?
Because why not? Just go!

Are dreams just tech support?
For our minds after dark?
Typing updates while we sleep,
In our brain's tech park!

As the Sun Sets on Certainty

As the sun dips low, doubts start to play,
Is there a manual for this craziness, I say?
Why do socks vanish in the laundry's domain?
Or are they plotting a sock rebellion in vain?

With maps in my head that seem to confuse,
Which way to the chocolate? I can't seem to choose.
Do fish ponder the ocean? It's hard to surmise,
Are they trapped in their depths, or living the highs?

In Search of Lost Certitudes

In wandering circles, I chase ghosts of thought,
Where's the key to wisdom that I swear I bought?
Did I lose it at dinner, or leave it at play?
Ah yes! It's with my sanity, hidden away!

Each question a riddle, wrapped up with a bow,
Why do we seek answers when we don't really know?
Is it true that the cake is a lie and a tease?
Or just a cruel joke from dear old life's wheeze?

Why Does the Night Speak?

At midnight, the moon whispers secrets of old,
Does it mock my anxieties, or is it just bold?
Are the stars all planners with too much free time?
Or do they just laugh as I'm stuck in my rhyme?

Why does the darkness give comfort and fright?
Can't it just stick to the rules in plain sight?
As shadows conspire in a dance of delight,
Is it laughter or tears in the hush of the night?

A Journey Through Unfinished Thoughts

On a quest for the answers, my pencil runs dry,
Do I write with my heart, or just wave it goodbye?
Paper cuts shuffle through the echoes of doubt,
Are they just reminders to laugh and to pout?

In a maze of reflections, I find humor's grace,
Why does pondering madness feel like a race?
Beware of the riddles that tickle the mind,
You might find more comfort in nonsense, so kind!

Is Happiness a Destination?

Is happiness a place to find,
Or just a state of the mind?
Do we pack bags, go on quests,
Or realize it's in silly jests?

Should we map it on Google Maps,
Or is it woven in belly laughs?
If I took a plane, what's the fare?
What's the baggage for joy we bear?

Maybe it's lost in a sock,
Or hiding beneath the tick-tock.
Maybe it's a pie on the sill,
Or a cat who just loves to chill.

So let's not stress on which road,
Just giggle and lighten the load.
Happiness might just be a joke,
One that bursts like a silly smoke.

How to Measure Joy?

Is joy a cup, filled to the brim,
Or a faint whisper, soft and dim?
Do we weigh it like sugar or gold,
Or is it laughter that can't be controlled?

Can we pour it in jars for the shelf,
Or must we find it deep in ourselves?
Is it found in a cake or a pie,
Or that silly moment you almost cry?

Do we count all the giggles in a day,
Or the number of times we forget to play?
Maybe joy's in a dance out of tune,
Or the sudden burst of a bright balloon.

Let's ditch the scales, toss out the charts,
Just listen for joy's funny little parts.
In giggles and wiggles, we can rejoice,
For joy is truly our playful choice.

The Paradox of Freedom

Is freedom a cage, with no door,
Or a wild dance on an open shore?
Can we escape while sipping our tea,
Or does freedom come with a fee?

Do we flee to find ourselves more,
Or is it in routine, like a chore?
Is the thrill in choices we make,
Or the comfort in not feeling fake?

Can it be small like a cat's little leap,
Or grand like promises we keep?
When we run, do we leave or we chase,
Or discover freedom's silly face?

So let's laugh as we ponder deep,
And maybe laugh ourselves to sleep.
In paradoxes, we find a clue,
Freedom's a riddle meant just for you.

When Do We Truly Know?

Is knowing a light that just flicks on,
Or a puzzle piece we put on?
Do we find it in wise, ancient books,
Or in the twinkle of friendly looks?

Is it a date that marks the score,
Or a feeling that asks for more?
Is knowing something that's vast and wide,
Or just a small guest we let stride?

Do we hold 'knowledge' tight, like a child,
Or let it run free—wild and riled?
When we think we know, do we find it's false,
Or just a wink in life's vast waltz?

So laugh when you think you've got it down,
For knowing's just twists of quirks in town.
In questions and giggles, we brush the clouds,
And celebrate knowing in vibrant crowds.

The Tug of Choices Unmade

A fork in the road, I pause to stare,
Do I want pizza or a salad to pair?
Decisions abound, my mind's like a maze,
Turning dinner into a baffling phase.

Should I wear blue or the bright shade of red?
Both look good, but which one's in my head?
Choices like socks, they seem to multiply,
Yet somehow I end up in the same old tie.

When Do We Truly Arrive?

Is it when you land, or when you unpack?
Is it the journey or the destination's knack?
Coffee in hand, do I finally behold?
Or is it just wishing for a place to unfold?

Oh, GPS says I've reached my end zone,
But it turns out it's just a new friend's phone.
With bags still jostling, who can define?
Arriving feels like a loopy design.

What Colors Paint Our Dreams?

In dreams, I'm a dragon; in life, just a man,
My fanciful hues slip like a cartoon plan.
From fuchsia to teal, what can they mean?
A mystery painting, born from a screen.

Pinks for the mornings when breakfast spills,
Greys for the hours when work just kills.
Each night I blend in shades bright and stark,
But wake up to see them fade to the dark.

Secrets of the Heart Unveiled

What's in there, a treasure, a pile of socks?
Or the secrets of life pinned down in a box?
I peek and I ponder, I giggle and frown,
Hiding my confessions in a whimsical gown.

I'm like a piñata, candy all over,
Bursting with truths, don't need a four-leaf clover.
If you dare take a swing, it's filled with delight,
Or you might just get old socks—a comical fright!

Retracing Footsteps into Destiny

Stumbled on my shoes today,
They whispered secrets of my way.
Each step a path I might not take,
Do I dance or just break?

Pavements cracked beneath my stride,
Should I laugh or just abide?
Maps and charts, I swipe and scroll,
But do they lead me to my goal?

The winds of fate swirl, oh my!
I check my compass, then I sigh.
Destiny's just a fancy guess,
With each wrong turn, I just digress.

But maybe joy's in not quite knowing,
Rolling with the punches, un-foreboding.
So here's to laughter, on this wild spree,
Tracing paths of absurdity!

Are We Here to Solve or to Wonder?

Rubix cubes in the sky,
When did we learn to ask why?
Pondering twinkling of the stars,
Here we are, bizarre avatars.

Math and science seem quite fair,
But can equations cure despair?
With laughter as my only tool,
Isn't it fun just to play the fool?

Philosophers in cozy chairs,
Overthinking cosmic affairs.
Grab a drink and join the chat,
While we poke fun at the format!

In a universe full of perplexing bliss,
Learning's fun, but let's not miss.
To wonder more than to resolve,
In chaos, life's quirks evolve!

The Space Where Thoughts Collide

In the realm of thoughts I roam,
My brain, a busy wifi zone.
Ideas bounce like frogs on logs,
Creating chaos, during the fog.

Questions leap and twist in air,
Why be normal? Why not dare?
With a giggle, I'll contemplate,
The mystery of my lunch plate.

Conversations swirling like a dance,
Funny riddles, given a glance.
From time to time, I lose my tread,
Is this brilliance, or just my head?

Through this space, we laugh and play,
Taking moments, joy on display.
In the madness, sparks ignite,
And confusion feels somewhat right!

Transitory Moments in Eternal Time

Catching glimpses like fireflies,
Moments flash, oh how they rise!
Tick-tock goes the clock's decree,
Yet here I stand, just sipping tea.

The past a ghost, the future hazed,
Life's a show, mildly phased.
I'm the star, or just the chair?
Is it a scene, or a fair affair?

Whispers of yesterday's glee,
Banter echoes, full of spree.
If this is fleeting, what's the crime?
I dance, forgetting the sweet climb.

So cherish now with all you own,
Laughing hearts don't stand alone.
In this drop of time divine,
Savor seconds with a glass of wine!

What Defines Us?

In a world of selfies, fame, and likes,
Do you measure worth by your food pics' spikes?
Is it the memes we share and spread?
Or how we dance in our pajamas instead?

What counts, the coffee or the buzz?
Or that time you swam with a shark because?
Do we define ourselves by our quirks?
Or the clumsy way we do our works?

Whispers Under a Starlit Sky

Under skies where dreams ignite,
Do nocturnal critters have thoughts that bite?
Does a star's twinkle hold a secret code?
Or is it just light putting on a show?

Do the stars gossip, or just blink at us?
About celestial couch potatoes, they discuss?
Can you ask a comet for advice?
Or is that just wishing on ice?

What Lingers Beyond the Veil?

Do ghosts clutch their phones and scroll with dread?
Wishing for likes from the long-dead?
What whispers in the wind when we ask?
"Did you send a tweet in that final task?"

Is it our snacks that haunt them at night?
Or does regret really take flight?
What lingers when the lights go out?
Is it laughter or just a shout?

Echoes of Tomorrow

Will tomorrow's echoes bring better memes?
Or just reruns of our craziest dreams?
Can we predict if cats will rule?
Or if humans'll act like the biggest fool?

What do we see in the crystal ball?
More cat videos or a doughnut stall?
Will our legacy be silly or grand?
Or just "that time we searched for lost band?"

The Space Between Choices

What to eat for lunch today?
Salad or pizza, come what may.
Greasy hands or leafy greens,
This choice is tougher than it seems.

Flip a coin, or ask a friend,
What's the worst that could descend?
A burger gone rogue, or fries with glee,
It's just food, who cares? Let's agree!

Why stress over paths we take?
Life's a game, make a mistake.
Jump right in, don't hesitate,
If all else fails, just celebrate!

Choices are like socks in drawers,
Match 'em up or just explore.
In the end, they don't define,
Just wear what's comfy, you'll be fine.

Reflections on Infinity

Time is a circle; oh what a trip!
It's a merry-go-round without a skip.
How many hours in a day?
Just enough for Netflix and play.

What's beyond the final star?
Did I leave the stove on? Oh, how bizarre!
Infinite thoughts racing my mind,
Yet I can't find my phone—oh, what a bind.

Maybe space is just a large joke,
The universe did giggle, then spoke.
If we're all stardust, take a bow,
I just hope I don't embarrass now.

So here's to pondering big things,
Like cats and their odd little flings.
Infinity's funny, like a bad pun,
Let's just laugh until we're done.

Can We Unravel the Unknown?

Is that a ghost in my fridge?
Or just leftovers I can't rid?
Unraveling things often brings dread,
So I'll just stick with the pizza instead.

Mysteries swirl like jellybeans,
What's the secret behind all machines?
Why is the toast always burnt?
These are things I've long since yearned.

Perhaps the answer's under the bed,
Next to my socks and some old bread.
But logic's hard, it's lost and found,
So let's dance like no one's around.

Unknowns are ripe with absurdity,
Like dogs who can't fathom gravity.
So here's to the chaos, wild and free,
May we embrace it with glee!

To Dream or Not to Dream

To sleep, perchance to dream tonight,
Will I float or take to flight?
What if I end up in a stew,
Just me and a giant kangaroo?

Dreams are wild, they seldom make sense,
Like a squirrel that plays the suspense.
But if I meet a dragon, oh dear,
Can I convince him to grab a beer?

Should I leap into slumber, take the dive?
Or binge-watch shows till I'm barely alive?
The struggle is real, what a tough plight,
Oh, what to do on this starry night?

So I'll toss and turn, what a scene,
Just to find out—was that a dream?
To dream or not? A question that's grand,
In the end, I'll just nap on demand.

Whispers of Existence

Why does toast always land sore?
Is gravity a punk, wanting more?
And if socks disappear in the wash,
Are they in a dance, or just a nosh?

Is the fridge reeling from our snacks?
Does it judge how often we relax?
Why do we all look so confused?
Especially when ice cream's abused?

Are ants a secret society?
Or just craftsmen of piety?
What if trees are really quite wise?
And they giggle when we don't realize?

Do we play hide and seek with fate?
And does destiny have a plate?
If laughter's the answer, what's the riddle?
We dance through nonsense, isn't it fiddled?

Where Do We Go from Here?

If coffee's a hug in a mug,
What's soda, a party drug?
Are sprinkles just confetti for cake?
Or fairy dust from a candy lake?

When cats have their meetings at night,
Do they plan a world filled with fright?
Or are they just plotting to steal
Our warmest spots, that's a big deal?

Is the universe lost in a maze?
With aliens taking a leisurely gaze?
If stars are simply holes in the dark,
Are wishes just farts that leave a spark?

Shall we dance in our pajamas at noon?
Or sing to the moon like a silly cartoon?
In the end, do we really care?
As long as we laugh with those who dare?

Echoes of the Unanswered

If time travel were real, I'd go back,
And tell my past self, 'Pick a better snack!'
If unicorns exist, where'd they go?
Probably hiding from a melted snow.

Do socks have a party in the dryer?
Playing games while my brain's on fire?
What's up with elevators and their doors?
Are they waiting to count down our chores?

Do goldfish dream of ocean floors?
Or just watch the world from their little stores?
In a land where questions bounce like balls,
Do we hear the echoes in empty halls?

If laughter's the key to the cosmic door,
What's the password? Tell me more!
In the end, let's tickle the truth,
With humor as our fountain of youth!

Threads of Uncertainty

Are we all just puppets on a string?
Or are we the dancers that chaos can bring?
Is the salad bowl just life's cruel trick?
Or do veggies sometimes get really thick?

Is my dog planning an escape?
With bunnies and squirrels, what's their shape?
If clouds wear pajamas to float,
Are we just ships in a whimsical boat?

Why do we never question our shoes?
Do they have plans we ought to peruse?
What if laughter is just a big chase?
Running in circles, it's life's funny race!

Shall we ponder what makes us tick?
Or embrace the absurd with a silly flick?
In the end, every smile and cheer,
Threads of uncertainty weave us near!

Moments Between the Stars

Is this sweater cosmic or just a mistake?
I can't decide if it's art or a gag.
In the dark, my dreams make sense,
Until morning laughs and pulls the tag.

Do aliens wear socks? I must know!
Do they sip tea or just float away?
In the vastness, my thoughts explode,
Like popcorn kernels on a sunny day.

Stars wink, thinking I'll figure it out,
But I'm still lost with my stale coffee.
Are we all just cosmic stand-up acts?
Tell me theories, or I might sneeze!

In this vast comedy, I'm just a clown,
With questions that tickle the brain.
So let's dance and laugh at the void,
As we float past celestial champagne.

The Weight of Choices

I stood at the crossroad, felt so weighty,
Deciding between pizza or a salad,
One makes me jiggle, the other—maybe,
But why is my face always so pallid?

Should I dive in or tiptoe around?
To risk it all or play it safe?
It's like picking which ice cream to sound
While my heart does an awkward waif.

Life's menu has two delicious sides,
But what if I want-thirds without fear?
I'll be the indecisive who confides,
In the flavor explosion of universal cheer!

So I'll order everything, spice up my fate,
With scoops of laughter and heaping grins.
Strawberry or chaos? Why contemplate?
Tomorrow's a buffet; let the feast begin!

Secrets in the Synapse

Electric whispers in my silly head,
Ideas jolt like jellybeans of thought.
Is it wisdom or a snack I need?
Let's binge on thoughts, endlessly caught!

Neurons dance like they just found a groove,
Twisting and turning in wild delight.
Where's the wisdom? Oh, it may prove
To be just a joke hiding out at night.

Plenty of secrets in the brain's nooks,
Like forgotten cookies in old, dusty books.
Craving the random, the bizarre, and strange,
In this game of neurons, I'm happy to exchange!

So let's toast to what we think we know,
And laugh as the synapses brighten our glare.
For within this jest, the wonders will flow,
With secrets that tickle, so light as air.

Time's Relentless River

Time flows like a river, oh what a drag,
With currents of worry and rocks of dread.
Do we paddle or just float with a bag?
Spilling drinks, laughing, tumbling instead!

Oh, the clocks tick like they're lost in a race,
Chasing seconds while I sip my tea.
Can I pause to take a good look at my case?
"Where's the manual for being carefree?"

With each splash, I'm soaking life's glee,
While alligators of doubt swim nearby.
But what's a river without a little spree?
Let's catch sunset waves and flirt with the sky!

So, here's to the laughter that washes ashore,
In this relentless rush, I'll still take a bow.
I'll build boats from my dreams, not to ignore,
As we wave at those rocks, with a mischievous vow!

Chasing Shadows of Truth

In a land where answers bounce,
I chase my shadows like a hound.
Questions hide behind the couch,
Lurking, laughing, all around.

I asked my sock about my fate,
It whispered back, 'You're just late!'
A crucial chat that now I know,
Turns out socks can steal the show.

Bananas ponder their own peel,
While apples ask, 'What is the feel?'
Mangoes giggle, 'Just be sweet!'
Nothing's ripe in this debate heat.

Maybe wisdom's found in jest,
A riddle wrapped in fruit, no less.
So let's all dance with goofy glee,
And chase those questions, wild and free!

When Time Becomes a Question

Tick tock, the clock just laughed,
As if it knows a precious craft.
I asked it once, 'What time is it?'
It said, 'Don't bother, have a fit!'

In the land of hourglass dreams,
I saw a snail racing, it seems.
'What's the rush?' I curiously asked,
'Time's a joke!' it gleefully tasked.

Calendars stare, confused, aghast,
Days go slow, then zoom on past.
A mystery wrapped in seconds tight,
All I know is snacks feel right.

So if you find yourself in doubt,
Remember to laugh and dance about.
Time's a question that can't be caught,
But joy? Now that's a whole new thought!

The Silence Between Heartbeats

In the hush where silence looms,
I think of cats, and all their zooms.
What is love? A purr or hiss?
An awkward pause, I guess that's bliss.

Heartbeat thumps like Morse code fun,
I wonder if my dog can run.
Looking deep into the still,
"Is that a cloud?" I hear the thrill.

Each silence carries quirky weight,
As if it's teasing, 'is this fate?'
My heart throws a quirky toss,
In moments strange, who's really boss?

So dance within that quiet space,
Twirl like confetti, don't lose pace.
For in the still, with giggles spry,
You'll find the truth in laughter, oh my!

Who Am I in the Mirror?

I looked and saw a face so strange,
It winked at me as if to change.
'Who are you?' I loudly cried,
But all I got was my own side.

Reflections chuckle, shadows sway,
Each morning brings this game to play.
Is that a hair, or just a bug?
Reality gives me a snug hug.

Mirrors speak in riddles, bright,
'You're a wonder! Now, take flight!'
But what if I'm just Mr. Blank?
A question marks his unknown rank.

With every glance, I giggle loud,
Embrace the odd, be quirky proud.
For who I am is a funky dance,
Each glance a chance to take a chance!

Melodies of an Unwritten Story

If I ask the moon for advice,
It just winks and rolls its eyes.
Coffee helps me ponder fate,
But breaks my heart at 6 AM late.

What's the secret to a good pie?
It's either love or store-bought lies.
The cat knows how to take its time,
As I rush at life like a clown in prime.

Is success just a well-timed sneeze?
Or a dance on top of golden trees?
The fish don't care if they can't fly,
While I'm stuck here wondering why.

So let's laugh as we trip and fall,
To find our voices in the squall.
An unwritten story still to sing,
In every misstep, joy takes wing.

Beneath the Layers of Existence

Why do we say that time is gold,
When it's just a number, far from old?
The universe shrugs at my plans,
While I'm stuck drawing life with crayons.

Do socks from the dryer really run?
Or do they just dream of the sun?
Each mystery leads to more questions,
Like why ice cream is a good suggestion.

If I ask a tree for wisdom tall,
Will it answer me with leaves that fall?
Or is my heart just a broken clock,
Ticking on feelings that no one talks?

Underneath it all, we simply seek,
A giggle in chaos, some joy to peek.
So let's dance on this cosmic stage,
Wearing our quirks like a badge of page.

Can Tomorrow Change Yesterday?

If I bake a cake just for today,
Will it make my past melt away?
With sprinkles of hopes and seeds of doubt,
I'm just a chef without a route.

Can I wear new sunglasses to see,
The past in a way that's more carefree?
Or will those moments just glare right back,
Like a dance floor with nothing to unpack?

If I could rewrite my biggest blunder,
Would it turn a frown to playful thunder?
Or am I just stuck in a comedy show,
With the same old jokes and a comedic woe?

Tomorrow laughs as it takes the stage,
While yesterday sulks in a quiet cage.
But I'll twirl in confusion, with cake in hand,
And let the sweet moments be well-planned.

Secrets Hidden in Plain Sight

The cat's a spy, that much is clear,
Watching my every one-man cheer.
The goldfish judging my daily snack,
As I stare at their bubbles in my pack.

Is the fridge a portal or just a door?
To snacks and leftovers that always bore?
That sock that went missing, where did it hide?
In a parallel world wearing a pink shade wide?

Can time be borrowed or only lent?
I'd pay it back with laughs well-spent.
As I search for meaning in silly things,
Like whether the chicken really has wings.

Under the sun, we giggle and play,
Finding treasures in the mundane fray.
So toast to the secrets that dance and flit,
In the chaos of life, here's to taking a hit.

Are We Just a Flicker?

Are we just sparks in the breeze?
Flashing bright, then gone with ease.
Can a moment truly last?
Or do we flicker, fading fast?

Ticking clocks and playful jests,
Living life as funny guests.
Are we shadows in a play?
Just a joke, then fade away?

Laughing loud at fate's design,
Are we merely light divine?
Dancing in the chance we take,
Or a joke that fate will make?

So let's spark and let it glow,
Dance like no one wants to know.
After all, what's really clear?
We're just flickers—bring the cheer!

The Nature of Belonging

Do I fit in, or am I odd?
Am I a peacock or a cod?
In circles wide with cards laid bare,
I ask if anyone could care?

Friends like socks that never match,
In this quirky, vibrant batch.
Am I the punchline to a joke?
Or the glue that keeps us stoked?

Shared glances in crowded rooms,
Do we bloom or just consume?
Together with my motley crew,
Do I belong? Who even knew?

So here's to all our strange appeals,
To the laughs and silly feels.
In this jigsaw, let's unite!
We're all strange—so hold on tight!

Embers of Possibility

In the ashes, warmth resides,
Dreams can spark and joy abides.
With a wish upon the night,
Can a flicker bring us light?

Every ember tells a tale,
Of the times that we mightail.
Like a magic that we hold,
What if it's worth more than gold?

Chasing dreams like fireflies,
Curious with open eyes.
Can the starlight hold our truth?
Or just fables from our youth?

So let's stoke those fiery beams,
Ignite our wildest hopes and dreams.
With laughter in each little spark,
We'll leave our mark—light up the dark!

Voices in the Void

Hello, is anyone out there?
Or is this just cosmic air?
Shouting loud into the hush,
Did I hear a giggle? Shush!

Echoes bounce without a face,
In the vastness, we find space.
Are these voices really mine?
Or a jest from the divine?

Questions float like misty air,
What's the point? Who really cares?
Is the void a home to jest?
Or do we simply fail the test?

So let's laugh at all we seek,
As the universe plays peek-a-boo.
In the void, we have to trust,
That we're all a little dust!

Will We Ever Truly Know?

Why did the chicken cross the road?
To find answers in the code!
But every turn just led to more,
Perhaps it's best to keep the score.

Are socks and shoes a cosmic pair?
Or just a myth beyond compare?
We ponder with a silly grin,
As mysteries keep piling in.

Why's every question lead to fun?
It's like chasing shadows on the run!
With queries bouncing all around,
Is knowledge lost, or maybe found?

So here we are, still asking why,
Just like a cat that's chasing sky!
We'll navigate this cosmic jest,
And laugh ourselves into the quest.

The Footprints of Our Choices

Footprints left on sandy shores,
Each step a tale, what's in store?
Do we step light or dance with grace?
Or just leave marks in silly places?

Choices made like candy sweet,
Some are bitter, some a treat.
But every choice brings giggles too,
Especially when they lead to you!

We ponder paths and weigh the scales,
Like curious detectives with our trails.
Will we forge a path or trip and fall?
Either way, we'll have a ball!

Our choices spark the wildest fun,
Like choosing ice cream over the bun!
With every footprint, laugh and cheer,
Embrace the chaos—never fear!

Are We The Sum of Our Questions?

Are we more than just our words?
Like shy little, fluttering birds?
Each question brings a curious smile,
Let's embrace the fun—it's worth the while!

What's the meaning of that old sock?
Or the time it felt like we'd unlock?
Each inquiry adds to our tale,
Like mixing flavors in a strange cocktail!

Are we wisdom wrapped in jest?
Or just a quest to find the best?
Questions swirl like clouds above,
With laughter as our daily love.

So ask away and let it flow,
In this circus, we steal the show!
Each question answered, more arise,
In this great pursuit, let's claim our prize!

The Whispering Threads of Time

Tick-tock goes the crafty clock,
What secrets hide within its rock?
Do minutes laugh and giggle too?
Or are they just a passing hue?

Threads of time weave tales so neat,
Like socks that vanish in the heat.
With each second, a chance to play,
As we bounce through night and day!

Whispers tell of futures bright,
Or of pizza at midnight's bite.
Can we twist or tangle fate?
Join the dance—let's celebrate!

So take a leap, embrace the ride,
With laughter on this time-tide!
Each tick, each tock, a story shared,
In this thread of laughs, we dared!

The Quest for Understanding

Why do socks disappear while we sleep?
Is the universe taking them in for a leap?
Do stars twinkle just for our glance?
Or is it space's way to dance?

Is the cake just a lie baked in grief?
Or does sugar hold secrets beyond belief?
Baking soda feels like the universe's trick,
Rising to heights, oh, so quick!

Can cats speak a language we've yet to find?
Or are they plotting to mess with our mind?
With their meows and their glare,
Do they chuckle while we declare?

Is it the journey that holds all the fun?
Or just the snacks when the day is done?
We pursue the weighty, the big, the grand,
But often it's just cookies in hand!

Fragments of Our Story

We sip our coffee, pondering 'Who am I?'
While debating if our toast should fly.
Are we stars caught in a gentle spin?
Or just dust bunnies beneath the din?

Does a sneeze mean a blessing or a curse?
Is it the universe's way to rehearse?
Perhaps it's a signal from celestial space,
To remind us the awkwardness is part of the race.

In the grand scheme, are we just a meme?
Life scrolling past like a webbed dream?
We laugh and we cry at the silly ol' fate,
But hand us a pizza and we'll celebrate!

When pondering meaning, we sometimes stray,
Into the fridge, 'What's for dinner today?'
So let's embrace the chuckles and snacks,
For in laughter, there are no cracks!

In the Silence of Thought

In silence, we wonder where lost keys go,
Do they join some secret agent's show?
Or are they just playing a prank?
While we search high and low, a big blank!

Why do we talk to ourselves so often?
When answers come back, are they Forgotten?
Perhaps there's wisdom in our own chatter,
Or just proof that we're really all scattered!

Does the fridge hum like a soothing tune?
Or is it plotting our midnight boon?
To lure us in with the glint of the light,
While we munch away, lost in delight!

With questions piling like dishes to scrub,
We wonder if Pandora's box is just a tub.
Rather than answers, let's grill up some fries,
For hunger, my friend, wears the wisest disguise!

Reflections in a Teardrop

Why do we cry at the silliest things?
Is it just our heart doing odd swings?
From movies that prompt a sweet sob,
To onions that tingle like a job!

Do butterflies dream of flying higher?
Or are they just fueled by birthday fire?
We ponder their freedom while stuck in our chairs,
But maybe they laugh at our silly stares!

Is time a trickster with its silly game?
Or just a friend with a really weird name?
We chase it down, but it slips away,
Laughing at us like we're in a play.

In reflections, we find both joy and pain,
Like rain on a sunny day—what a gain!
So let's dance with the quirks that we meet,
And savor the flavors of all that's sweet!

The Art of Letting Go

Balloons float high, we wave goodbye,
Worry's a weight, so let it fly.
Your ex called, it's just a test,
Drop the baggage and feel your best.

Dust bunnies dance in empty rooms,
Chasing dreams, avoiding gloom.
A fridge full of leftovers waits,
Just let go, don't tempt your fates.

Socks get lost in the drier's whirl,
Hold no grudges, give life a twirl.
Laughter's the key to letting be,
Freedom's found in comedy.

With each release, the heart grows light,
Letting go is pure delight.
Like a sneeze in the middle of work,
Embrace the chaos; it's how we lurk.

Embracing the Unknown Embrace

What lies ahead? A cosmic joke?
Curiosity twists, like a yoke.
An open mind is full of cheer,
What if the weird is what draws near?

Maps are nice, but who needs a guide?
Turn left at the funny, take it in stride.
Adventure calls with a funny tune,
Dance like nobody's watching, afternoon!

Peeking behind each shadowy door,
Confetti thoughts—who could ask for more?
Life's a mystery wrapped in a pun,
Embrace the unknown; it's all in fun.

So what's the next step? Just take a leap!
The unknown is where wild dreams creep.
Laugh at the odd and weirdly divine,
Each twist is just fine; it's all part of the design.

Halos of Questions Long Forgotten

Why are ducks so cool and wise?
Do they ever wear a big surprise?
Questions float like clouds in space,
Chasing answers at a breakneck pace.

What if cats hold secret lore?
And nightly meetings behind closed doors?
A world of queries wrapped in smiles,
Searching for wisdom across the miles.

Do plants feel joy or just the sun?
Do fish ever wish for a little fun?
What if gravity's just a prank?
Halos of laughter in the cosmic flank?

Perhaps the answers lie in jest,
Laughter's the prize; it's surely the best.
Embrace the weirdness, let go of dread,
In questions' arms, we joyfully tread.

What Happens at the Crossroads?

Two paths meet; flip a coin,
Heads for pizza, tails enjoy some groin.
Confusion swaggers in a funky hat,
Life spins around like a dance mat.

Decisions wait with a playful grin,
Should I be sensible or give in?
Taking a chance is the way to go,
Let the road less traveled steal the show.

What if I choose the wrong direction?
A story awaits in each connection.
Maybe unicorns will greet me there,
With pizzas and cotton candy to share.

So at the crossroads, shake off your fears,
Jump in the car; let's shift those gears.
Life's a circus; let's take the ride,
And follow our laughter wherever it glides.

The Weight of an Asterisk

Why'd I sign that contract, oh dear?
Just noticed an asterisk hiding here.
It mentions a fee, an odd little twist,
Did I really need to check that list?

Life comes with clauses, what a twist!
I missed the fine print, can't believe I wished.
An asterisk dancing, playing a game,
Now I'm stuck here, feeling the shame.

Terms and conditions, why are you sly?
I might trade my car for a pie in the sky.
Yet here I sit, with bills in my hand,
Next time I'll read, won't be so unplanned.

In this grand circus, I laugh at my fate,
Contracts and asterisks, oh, isn't it great?
I'll just chalk it up to a comedy show,
Next time, I'll wear my reading glasses, though!

Threads of Fate in the Cosmic Weave

What if my fate's trapped in a sock?
Worn at the toe, it just mocks.
Spun from the loom of cosmic glee,
I guess I'll just sip my chamomile tea.

Destiny's thread tangles in the wash,
Pairing socks with an unusual posh.
One bright and one dark, where's my mate?
A fashion disaster, oh isn't that great?

Grand visions of stars, or just an odd string?
Why must the universe make my head spin?
Is there a pattern or just a big mess?
Maybe that's fate's way to impress!

With laughter and whim, I'll take a bold leap,
Even if my socks make me weep.
In this cosmic dance, I twirl and I sway,
Who knew my fate resided in disarray?

What Lies Beyond the Horizon?

What lies beyond that distant screen?
Is it ice cream? Or a marketing scheme?
A mirage of tacos, floating so high,
Just out of reach, why can't I fly?

The horizon grins, holding its secrets tight,
I squint in the sun, filled with delight.
Is it fame, a treasure, or just more fuss?
Or merely a bus full of guys named Gus?

As I wander the shores with a thirst for more,
Each wave a question, crashing the shore.
Will I find fortune in that strange rise?
Or just a sandcastle that crumbles and dies?

Yet forward I march with a curious glance,
Ready to follow that whimsical dance.
For what lies beyond is just a red herring,
Or maybe the start of my new paring!

Echoes of Yesterday's Promises

Oh, the promises made back in the day,
Now echo like ghosts in a humorous way.
"Lose ten pounds," I said with a cheer,
But the pizza delivery guy just appeared here!

Promises fade like old photographs,
Each one a reminder of epic gaffs.
"Save for tomorrow!" chimes my old brain,
But tomorrow, it seems, comes with more gain!

Echoes of wisdom, what do they tell?
Don't trust a scale or an old fortune tell.
For laughter's my guide, through thick and thin,
Rocking this journey, let the giggles begin!

So here I stand, amidst yesterday's lies,
Smiling and laughing, watching the skies.
What's done is done, let the past just be,
The best promise, perhaps, is just being me!

Navigating Through the Fog of Doubt

Why is it hard to choose my path?
The GPS just shows me a laugh.
Do I take a left? Or a right?
Maybe I'll just stay in tonight.

Thoughts are clouds blocking the sun,
Do I run or should I just stun?
Each decision feels like a guess,
At least I can blame the stress.

Wisdom often comes too late,
When you ponder 'bout your fate.
With every turn and twist I take,
I wonder if I've made a mistake.

Tangled up in what I think,
Life feels more like a sink.
Questions swirling in my brain,
But hey, at least I'll entertain!

Is Hope a Illusion or a Light?

Hope's a flicker, burning small,
A joke on walls that might just fall.
Is it real or just a tease?
Sometimes I just laugh and sneeze.

In the daytime, it shines bright,
At night, it's just an eerie fright.
Does it guide or pull the strings?
Like a cat with broken wings.

Poking fun at thought's cruel jest,
Maybe hope's a cosmic test.
Oh! Will it last or fade away?
Onward, I chuckle, come what may.

Is it bright or just my sight?
Is it wrong, or could it be right?
I'll just watch as thoughts collide,
And laugh while hope takes me for a ride!

Conversations with the Universe

Hey there, Universe, what's your plan?
Why am I stuck in this traffic jam?
Is it fate or pure silly chance?
Can we chat? I'd like to dance.

Stars still wink through the thick haze,
Do they see my endless maze?
I asked for signs, but got a meme,
Do you hear me? Or is this a dream?

What's the answer to my woes?
The more I seek, the less it flows.
The cosmos laughs at all my plight,
Let's grab a drink while we unite.

Oh, dear stars, let's share a laugh,
Are you my guide? Or just my math?
In this vast void, I seek a clue,
But I'm still waiting for a view!

The Quicksand of Regrets

Regrets are like a sticky pit,
You jump right in - oh, what a hit!
Every choice seems a wrong turn,
But they're just lessons for me to learn.

Sitting here, I scratch my head,
What if I took a path instead?
The 'what-ifs' slip away so fast,
Instead of dwelling on the past.

Regrets giggle like old friends,
A comedy act that never ends.
With every mistake I tend to make,
I find more ways my heart can ache.

Can I laugh or just retreat?
Stuck in this trap that feels so sweet.
But hey, I'll dance on this quicksand stage,
Turning regrets into funny rage!

Patterns in the Cosmic Dance

Stars twirl in a jazzy spree,
Like disco balls on a cosmic spree.
Planets spin with groovy flair,
Who knew space had such wild hair?

Gravity's just a heavy beat,
Pulling us down to our own feet.
Moonwalkers in the lunar night,
All trying to dance with delight!

Asteroids drift like lost dancers,
Comets flashing, taking chances.
What's the rhythm of the spheres?
Or just science having cheers?

In this show of cosmic play,
Are we the stars or just cliché?
Finding fun in the vast unknown,
Laughing all while the seeds are sown.

How Far Can We Stretch Infinity?

Infinity's not a rubber band,
Yet we stretch it with a wink and stand.
Can we reach it through this phone?
Scroll forever, feel like home?

Time loops back like a poodle's hair,
Chasing tails, it doesn't care.
Is the universe just one big joke?
Or is it bored and needs a poke?

Twinkle, twinkle, endless light,
How far can we stretch this flight?
Past the stars, or just to Mars?
Maybe we should ask the cars.

In cosmic jest, we whirl and twirl,
Finding humor in every swirl.
With laughter echoing through the void,
Who knew infinity's a bit paranoid?

The Language of Stars

Stars whisper secrets on high,
Do they giggle as they fly?
Constellations have a chat,
Trading jokes like tit for tat.

Shooting stars fall with flair,
Are they just trying to scare?
What do they say when they meet?
'Hey, buddy, this is lit and neat!'

Galaxies swirl with riotous glee,
Language lost, yet so carefree.
Black holes mumble—what was that?
Did you hear the cosmic splat?

In the silence, stars laugh bright,
Playing hide and seek all night.
In this play of cosmic art,
Do they know they steal our heart?

Reflections on the Edge of Time

Time is a mirror holding fun,
Reflecting what we've said and done.
Do we age like fine old cheese?
Or just get caught up in the sneeze?

Seconds tick like clumsy feet,
Falling over, can't compete.
Do minutes giggle as they pass?
Or do they just drop a glass?

Years roll by in silly chains,
Maybe they're playing games.
Should we dance on time's great edge,
Or just join a wobbly hedge?

On this ride without a map,
Does time know it's a funny chap?
At the edge, we laugh and chime,
Just reflections on the edge of time.

What If the Journey Is the Answer?

What if the signposts are wrong, you see?
A road trip to nowhere is still quite a spree.
We chase all the wrong stuff in shiny cars,
But the best sights are often free under the stars.

Would we really want all the answers so bright?
Guessing's the game that keeps us up at night.
We laugh at our maps, oh what a hoot,
While the GPS insists we take a new route.

Mistakes are just laughs in the grand scheme of fate,
Each wrong turn a story, much better than straight.
Stopovers in life, where we pick up some cheer,
Here's to the chaos that makes it all clear!

So let's roll the dice, spin around in delight,
Collect all the weirdness, make wrongs feel so right.
Every bump in the road is a dance we can do,
The joy's in the journey, not just in the view!

Can We Dance with Doubt?

Can we tango with doubt, take a leap in the air?
Or are we just shuffling, pretending to care?
In a waltz with our worries, we step on our toes,
But with laughter, we've mastered this dance of woes.

A jitterbug twist turns our fears into fun,
We'll boogie to questions till the night is done.
Doubt may lead us, but we'll not hit the floor,
With rhythm and grace, we can always encore!

Can we juggle our dreams, while we shimmy with stress?

Each stumble is part of our fabulous mess.
Let's cha-cha with courage, while donning a grin,
Doubts don't stand a chance; let the party begin!

So let's sway through uncertainty, hand in hand,
We'll dive in the madness and dance on the sand.
When doubts try to lead, let's just add some flair,
With humor and moves, doubts won't dare to scare!

The Palette of Experience

With brushes in hand, we swirl every hue,
Life's canvas is messy, but oh, how it's true!
We splash on the laughter, then let sorrow run,
Every moment a stroke, telling tales in the sun.

From pastel adventures to dark shades of doubt,
Every splash of confusion can teach us about.
Mistakes are just colors we blend in with glee,
The palette of life: a wild jubilee!

Add in a dash of wild whimsy and cheer,
When the paint starts to bubble, we know we're near.
The masterpiece waits, though we never quite know,
What the final picture will show when we go.

So let's mix up our stories, keep painting the skies,
In this gallery of moments, surprise never lies.
For each stroke of confusion brings laughter anew,
With the palette of experience, we craft what is true!

Flickering Candles of Understanding

In a room full of candles, they dance all around,
Each flame tells a story that's waiting, profound.
We squint through the shadows, searching for light,
Stops and starts of insight, oh, what a sight!

Some candles burn brightly, while others just hum,
But each little flicker is where wisdom will come.
Trying to grasp it can feel quite absurd,
Yet trying keeps us laughing with what we have heard.

Let's gather our candles, set fires aglow,
We'll toast to confusion, already we know!
With each silly question, like wax they may drip,
But the laughs that we share are the sweetest of sips.

So let's light up the room with our quirks and our jest,
Finding warmth in the chaos will always be best.
Flickering candles, we gather and cheer,
Here's to the chuckles that fill us with cheer!

Stirring the Pot of Consciousness

Why do socks always disappear?
Left with a shoe and a tear.
Is it fate or a sock thief's thrill?
Maybe they're off for a sock-filled chill.

Do we exist beyond our fears?
Or just chase dreams with flowing beers?
Do we really need to know why?
Perhaps it's just to eat pie and sigh.

What if this is just a game?
A cosmic joke or just plain lame?
Can we rewrite our fated tale?
Or do we simply bark and wail?

Every thought, a noodle in soup,
Stir it well; join the happy troupe.
Does pondering matter in the night?
Or is it just a silly fight?

Beyond the Horizon of Self

What's beyond the mirror's gaze?
Perhaps an octopus in a daze.
Are we just cells, a cosmic game?
Or are we all searching for fame?

Do we float on clouds made of fluff?
Or sip coffee when things get tough?
If I'm me, and you're you—woo!
Who decides what's fake or true?

Can a cat teach us to be wise?
With those sly and sparkling eyes.
Are we just stardust with a grin?
Or are we hiding beneath our skin?

Why fret so much about the past?
When life's a riddle, not meant to last.
So dance a bit and take a twirl,
Embrace the chaos; give it a whirl!

Are We More Than Our Designs?

Are we just pixels on a screen?
Or thoughts that merge like cream and bean?
Is there more than fashion's glare?
Or are we just chasing the latest hair?

What do our profiles really show?
A curated life, or just a low blow?
If I change the filter, am I new?
Or still me, wearing the same old shoe?

Can a doodle tell of who I am?
Or just a quirky little glam?
Are we more than what we wear?
Or bound to fashion's fickle snare?

So laugh at trends, they come and go,
Life's a party, not a show.
Let's paint outside the lines we see,
Because the canvas is wild and free.

Fragments of a Wandering Soul

Is this a quest or just a stroll?
Am I the driver or just the scroll?
Do I seek gold, or just a muse?
Or simply wonder what's in the snooze?

Are we echoes from the past?
Whispering truths, or shadows cast?
Do we follow the maps we draw?
Or are we just here to play and gnaw?

Every question a fleeting spark,
Lighting shadows where we embark.
Can wisdom hide in a puppy's gaze?
Or is it lost in a goofy phase?

So here's to wandering, nothing planned,
Searching the universe, hand in hand.
With laughter, love, and a splash of soul,
Let's piece together this wobbly whole.

The Map of Unanswered Whys

Why do socks disappear, oh where do they roam?
The dryer's got secrets, it feels like a tome.
Do cats plot world takeovers, we can't quite tell?
They stare with such purpose, in their cozy shell.

Is cheese a food group, or just for delight?
And why can't the moon come out in daylight?
Do plants feel lonely when we're not around?
They whisper sweet nothings, but it's not profound.

Why is it so hard to find the remote?
It's lost in the couch, like it took a boat.
Do fish have their meetings, discussing the wave?
Or are they just swimming, so clueless and brave?

If pigeons could talk, what tales would they weave?
Of bread crumb betrayals and plans to deceive?
What are we all doing? Who really knows?
Just laughing and wondering as time quickly goes.

Whispers of the Unseen Forces

What's that sound in the night? Is it just my cat?
Or ghosts in the attic, plotting a chat?
Do shadows have feelings, or just play along?
They dance in the corners, it feels like a song.

Why do we all trip on invisible stones?
While thinking of galaxies and distant drones?
Are squirrels the spies of the urban terrain?
Collecting our secrets, oh what a campaign!

Does anyone know why toast hits the floor?
It lands buttered side down, and begs for more.
Is caffeine our fuel, or just a cruel prank?
We joke about health, while we wish for the bank.

Where do all the lost keys go to conspire?
In a secret lair, fueled by desire?
What's really in dreamland, a whimsical land?
A playground for thoughts, all made out of sand.

In Pursuit of Elusive Truths

Why do we yawn when we see someone else?
Are we mimicking boredom, or hiding ourselves?
Is pizza a circle? Or just happy pie?
Why's every good joke deserve a pie in the eye?

Can fish ever swim in a circle of thought?
Or is that a human trait that we've all sought?
Do trees have a gossip of who's thick or thin?
They lean in together, then whisper and grin.

Why do we always run from honest sights?
Yet binge-watch our lives as reality bites?
Is laundry a monster that breeds in the dark?
It eats all our socks, but leaves us in spark.

What's truly the meaning of "just one more snack?"
A question of hunger, or a fun little hack?
Is there wisdom in craziness, a spark in the jest?
Or do clowns know the answers that we never guessed?

The Recipe of Our Existence

What's in the recipe that makes us feel whole?
Is it love, or just cookies that play a big role?
A dash of adventure, a pinch of the weird,
Stir it up with some laughter, make sure it's not smeared.

Do we mix up our futures like batter in bowls?
Or wing it with frosting, just flirting with goals?
Why does time seem to vanish when life's so absurd?
It tickles and giggles, no word can be heard.

How do we season our days with some joy?
Is it simply the moments we choose to enjoy?
A sprinkle of kindness, a hint of some fun,
Are we all just ingredients, under one sun?

Why do we ponder the things that we crave?
Are we meant to be puzzled, or daringly brave?
With our forks held up high, let's whip up a cheer,
For the recipe's messy, but that makes it sincere.

www.ingramcontent.com/pod-product-compliance
Lightning Source LLC
Chambersburg PA
CBHW051649160426
43209CB00004B/850

* 9 7 8 1 8 0 5 6 6 1 5 8 0 *